GLADIATORS
AND THE STORY
OF THE COLOSSEUM

By
Dr. Nicholas Saunders

School Specialty
Publishing

Columbus, Ohio

Emperor Vespasian A.D. 9–79. Vespasian became Roman Consul in A.D. 51. In A.D. 66, he was given command of the war against the Jews by Emperor Nero. In A.D. 69, after the death of Nero and a period of confusion in Rome, Vespasian's legions claimed him as emperor. He began the Flavian dynasty. He started rebuilding Rome, which included the Colosseum.

Emperor Titus A.D. 39-81. The son of Vespasian, Titus took over the war against the Jews and besieged Jerusalem. He became emperor after his father's death in A.D. 79. Titus also continued the rebuilding of Rome. Titus completed the Colosseum, which he opened with 100 days of celebrations in A.D. 80.

Priscus and Verus They were two evenly matched gladiators who were featured in one of the contests that Emperor Titus organized to open the Colosseum. The crowd and EmperorTitus greatly appreciated their skill and their hard-fought contest, in which neither could defeat the other. Both the spectators and the emperor decided on a draw. Titus rewarded both men with riches and palms to commemorate their joint victory.

Emperor Commodus A.D. 161-192. Commodus was a great supporter of gladiatorial contests and fought many times in the Colosseum in carefully orchestrated fights that he always won. During these contests, he also killed thousands of animals, such as elephants, giraffes, leopards, and ostriches. He was eventually strangled in his bath by a servant.

Emperor Constantine (Constantine the Great) A.D. 271-337. Born a pagan, Constantine became emperor in A.D. 307. He converted to Christianity in A.D. 312. He announced that Christianity was the empire's only official religion. Constantine made the old Greek city of Byzantium (in modern Turkey) his new capital of Constantinople—a move that began the gradual demise of Rome and the Colosseum.

School Specialty Publishing

CONTENTS

THE ROMAN EMPIRE

In A.D. 100, the Roman Empire was at its height, stretching from Hadrian's Wall in northern Britain to Egypt and Mesopotamia (modern Iraq) in the east. Millions of people across the Mediterranean were part of the empire, and Rome was the richest and most powerful city in the ancient world.

Hadrian's wall
NORTH SEA
BALTIC SEA
BRITAIN
• London
GERMANIA
ATLANTIC OCEAN
GAUL
DALMATIA
DACIA
• Milan
BLACK SEA
ITALY
THRACE
IBERIA
MACEDONIA
• Rome
• Byzantium
ASIA MINOR
• Actium
ANATOLIA
MESOPOTAMIA
• Gades
• Campania
• Ephesus
Cyprus
• Carthage
Crete
Rhodes
SYRIA
CYRENE
MEDITERRANEAN SEA
NORTH AFRICA
Alexandria
• Jerusalem
LIBYA
EGYPT
ARABIA

☐ Roman Empire

Roman civilization was greatly influenced by the earlier Etruscan civilization, which had ruled Rome until 509 B.C. The Etruscans' funeral traditions involved fighting contests and human sacrifice in honor of the spirits of the dead. These rituals were the origins of Rome's gladiatorial contests

Examples of gladiators were recorded during the 4th century B.C. among the Samnite people from Campania, south of Rome. The Samnites became the models for the Roman gladiators that appeared fifty years later.

Rome's Colosseum was based on earlier and much smaller amphitheaters, where games, executions, animal hunts, and gladiatorial contests were held. After the Colosseum was built, many older amphitheaters were demolished and rebuilt in the style of the Roman Colosseum.

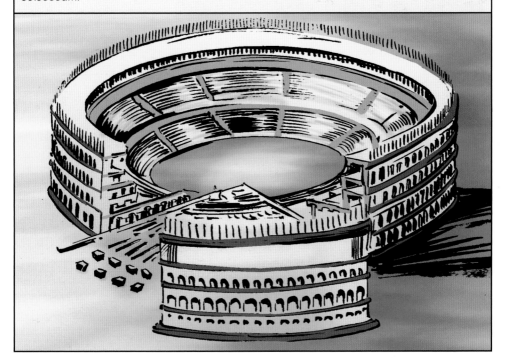

VISION OF THE COLOSSEUM

In A.D. 69, the Roman general Vespasian became emperor. He began planning the Colosseum as part of his large-scale rebuilding of Rome's grand architecture. The site he chose was occupied by the ornamental lake and the Golden House that the previous emperor, Nero, had constructed.

COLOSSEUM

OLD CITY WALLS

PLAN OF ROME

After years of waiting, and after having fought many hard wars throughout the empire, Vespasian finally became emperor when Nero died and his successors were murdered.

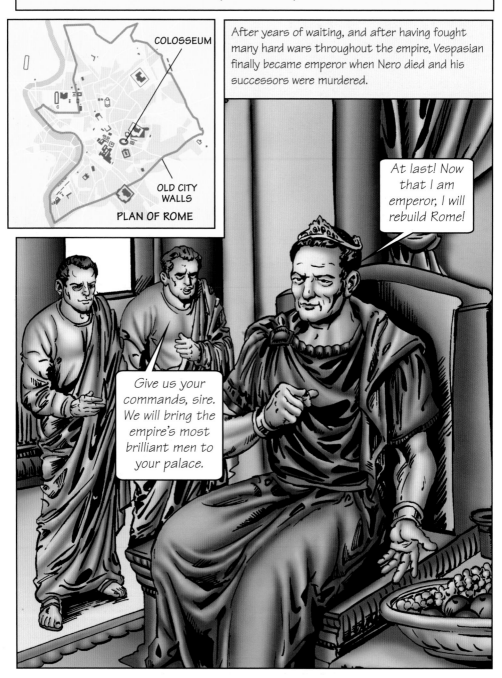

At last! Now that I am emperor, I will rebuild Rome!

Give us your commands, sire. We will bring the empire's most brilliant men to your palace.

After the chaos and confusion of Nero's reign, Vespasian decided to repair and rebuild the center of imperial Rome. He spent vast sums of money on his new constructions. He decided to build the Colosseum as the empire's largest amphitheater.

It would be a great honor.

I want you to design and build the largest amphitheater in the empire in the center of Rome.

Roman workmen labored tirelessly to turn Vespasian's plans into reality. They dismantled Nero's Golden House, stone by stone, to make way for the Colosseum's foundation.

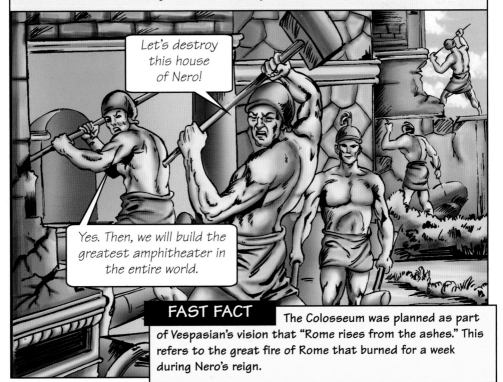

Let's destroy this house of Nero!

Yes. Then, we will build the greatest amphitheater in the entire world.

FAST FACT The Colosseum was planned as part of Vespasian's vision that "Rome rises from the ashes." This refers to the great fire of Rome that burned for a week during Nero's reign.

Nero's large ornamental lake in the gardens adjacent to the Golden House was drained to provide more space for the Colosseum.

We must empty Nero's lake to make more room for Vespasian's building.

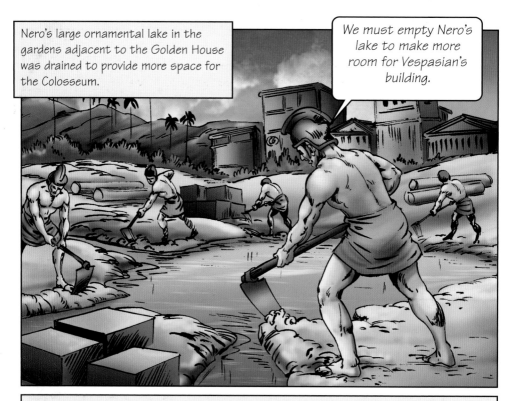

When the whole area had been cleared, Vespasian's architects and workmen laid the Colosseum's foundation. The first level was built with travertine, concrete, and marble. The stonework was joined together with iron clamps.

These are the largest blocks of travertine we have ever worked with. This amphitheater will last a thousand years!

In A.D. 79, Vespasian died before the Colosseum was completed. His son, Titus, became emperor and completed the building of the immense amphitheater.

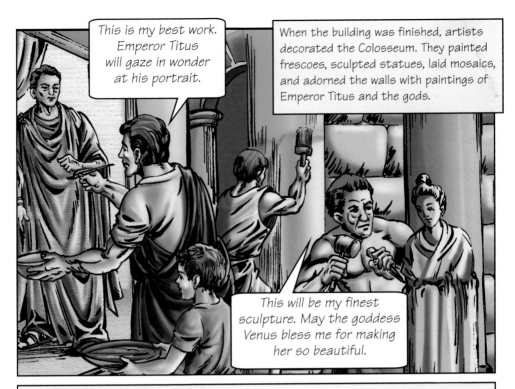

This is my best work. Emperor Titus will gaze in wonder at his portrait.

When the building was finished, artists decorated the Colosseum. They painted frescoes, sculpted statues, laid mosaics, and adorned the walls with paintings of Emperor Titus and the gods.

This will be my finest sculpture. May the goddess Venus bless me for making her so beautiful.

In A.D. 80, Emperor Titus opened the Colosseum with 100 days of special events held throughout the city.

See how the amphitheater is filling up? If only my father, Vespasian, were here to see it.

The completed Colosseum had special boxes for the emperor and his family, entrances at different levels, and awnings that could be stretched over part of the arena to shade the spectators from the sun.

The opening ceremony at the Colosseum began with traitors being paraded in front of the emperor and then banished from Rome.

Rome's greatest amphitheater will be open with the banishment of the city's traitors!

Kill the beast! Spear it now!

The next event was the slaughter of animals in the arena. As many as 5,000 bears, lions, tigers, giraffes, rhinoceroses, and wild pigs were killed on the opening day. Many more animals were killed during the following months.

Yaaaghh!

Gladiatorial contests followed. Two gladiators, Priscus and Verus, fought long and hard with skill and daring, but were equally matched.

Come Priscus, do your best!

You fight well Verus, but I will defeat you!

No winner emerged, so Titus decided that both men were champions and awarded each the symbols of victory—a palm branch and a laurel wreath.

We are both champions! Neither could defeat the other!

FAST FACT Executions disguised as re-enactments of ancient myths were part of the Colosseum's opening entertainment. The myth of Orpheus, who charmed animals to lie down beside him by playing the flute, was staged. In the Colosseum, however, instead of lying down next to the man, the bear mauled him.

Many gladiators were prisoners of war captured during Roman victories across the empire—from Britain to Iberia (Spain), and from Greece to Asia Minor (modern Turkey).

Your fate is sealed, soldier. You will be taken to Rome to be sold as a slave or to fight as a gladiator.

Some gladiators were thieves arrested in the market places of Rome and other imperial cities. They were punished by being sold to a gladiator school.

Grab that man, soldier. He's a thief!

Some gladiators actually came from high-class Roman society. Infatuated with the glamour of fighting in the Colosseum, well-born young men would volunteer to become gladiators. They paid for their own training and received the helmets and weapons of their new trade. They were treated as any other gladiator.

Do you really want to exchange your soft life for the blood and sweat of the arena?

Yes, procurator. I dream of fighting in the Colosseum.

Occasionally, women became gladiators. They were especially popular among the Roman crowds. Several women fought during the first contests at the Colosseum in A.D. 80.

Roman women can fight as well as any man!

Roman crowds loved to see different kinds of gladiators fighting each other. A favorite contest was between the retiarius—armed with only a trident and net—and a Thracian, who wore a crested helmet and fought with a curved sword and small shield.

Mounted gladiators were called *equites*. They wore helmets with visors and carried small circular shields. They would begin their fights on horseback, but then dismount to finish the contest on foot.

"See how these British barbarians fight!"

"Aaaaghhh!"

One type of gladiator was the essedarius, who fought while driving a chariot. The idea probably came from the Roman army's battles against chariot-riding British warriors. Essedarius contests became popular after the conquest of Britain.

Spectacular gladiatorial contests also occurred between the lightly armed Secutor, who wore a helmet and carried a short sword and a large, rectangular shield, and the Hoplomachus, a heavily-armed gladiator. The Hoplomachus wore a crested helmet and armor, and he fought with a round shield and sword.

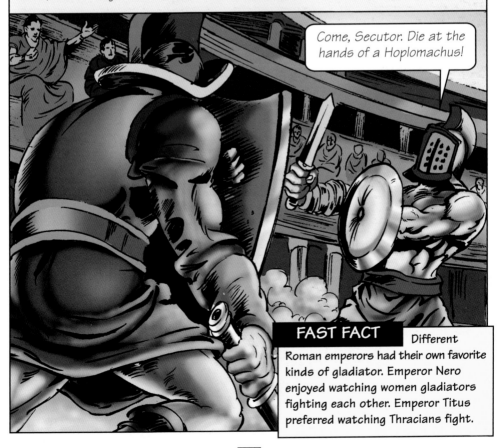

Come, Secutor. Die at the hands of a Hoplomachus!

FAST FACT Different Roman emperors had their own favorite kinds of gladiator. Emperor Nero enjoyed watching women gladiators fighting each other. Emperor Titus preferred watching Thracians fight.

A GLADIATOR IS CHOSEN

Young gladiators were sometimes prisoners of war, captured during Roman conquests across the empire. Some were natural fighters, whose training in the gladiator schools sharpened their skills. These young champions often defeated experienced gladiators at the Colosseum and became famous celebrities in Roman society.

A young prisoner of war would be chained to a chariot and paraded through the streets of Rome.

The young man would then be given a choice—either to be a household slave, or to train as a gladiator for the Colosseum. If the youth decided to be a gladiator, the Roman officer sold him to the procurator of Ludus Magnus, the gladiator training school near the Colosseum.

You have a choice, young man. Be sold as a house slave or win fame and freedom as a gladiator.

I will take my chances in the Colosseum.

Gladiators were trained at a gladiator school for the next few years.

Here is the gold we agreed to pay for the young man.

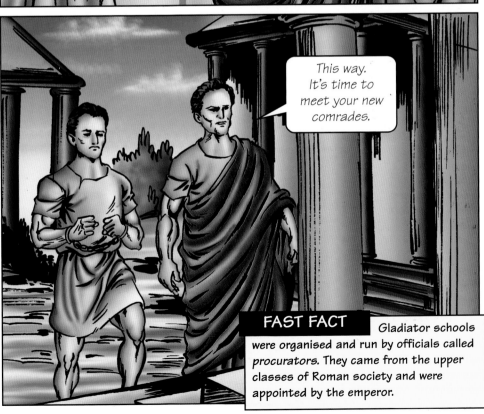

This way. It's time to meet your new comrades.

FAST FACT Gladiator schools were organised and run by officials called procurators. They came from the upper classes of Roman society and were appointed by the emperor.

Every day, a young gladiator would train with other more experienced men to learn the art of fighting as entertainment for the Colosseum's spectators.

Yaahhh! I am getting the idea now.

See, like this! This is a killing blow.

Often, the climax of a gladiatorial contest was the final kill. The lanista taught the trainees how to cut an opponent's jugular vein.

The lanista, or trainer, taught young gladiators about the weak spots of the body, showing which blows would wound and which would kill. This enabled gladiators to pace their fights for the spectators' enjoyment.

Uuuughh! You will never win like that!

Once ready, a young gladiator built up his strength and courage by first killing a chained lion.

During this period, wild beasts from all over the Roman Empire were brought to Rome to be killed in the Colosseum.

In his first public show in the Colosseum, a young gladiator might appear as a retiarius, armed with only a trident and net.

Aaghhhh! Somebody help me!

Monster, feel the spikes of my trident!

During a morning contest, a gladiator might fight large crocodiles brought from the Nile River in Egypt.

Other animals in the arena included ostriches. They were fought with a crescent-shaped blade.

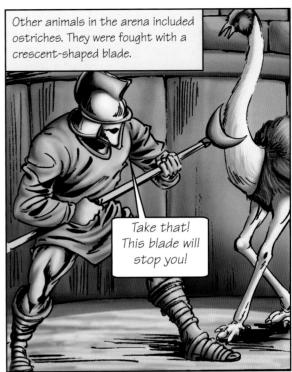

Take that! This blade will stop you!

Hail to the emperor!

If a young gladiator pleased the crowd, they would let him know by cheering their approval at the end of the contest.

Watch my net, beast! Here is my trident!

Once gladiators had fighting experience in the arena, they would soon face really ferocious creatures, such as huge bears brought from Germany. Animals, such as bears, required the bestiarii to fight much more skillfully.

You are quick, young man!

If a gladiator could defeat wild beasts, he was then allowed to fight his first human opponent.

A young gladiator could use his energy and strength to defeat more experienced fighters, such as this equite, or gladiator on horseback.

Gladiators without body armor used skill and agility to outmaneuver and kill heavily-armed opponents, much to the amusement of the Colosseum's watching crowd.

FAST FACT Roman crowds loved to see contests between different kinds of gladiators so that they could appreciate the skills of each type. The crowds especially enjoyed a fight where a lightly-armed gladiator, such as a retiarius, defeated a more heavily-armed opponent, such as a Hoplomachus.

A GLADIATOR'S LIFE

The glamor and glory of being a successful gladiator gave the best fighters a good lifestyle when they were not fighting in the amphitheater. They were sometimes rewarded by the emperor, particularly Emperor Commodus, who was obsessed with the gladiatorial and animal-hunt shows staged in the Colosseum.

If a young gladiator gained a good reputation quickly, he would meet with the procurator of the training school. The procurator would discuss future fights and how a fighter's career should develop.

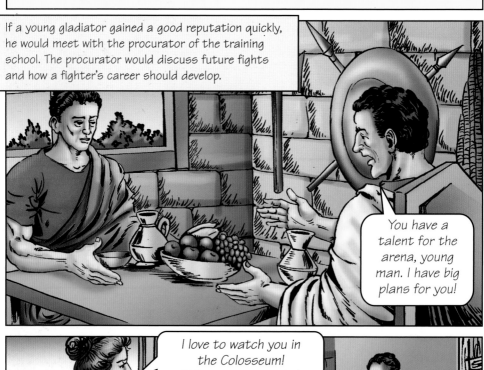

You have a talent for the arena, young man. I have big plans for you!

I love to watch you in the Colosseum! Tell me your secrets!

I have had the very best training, my lady.

Successful gladiators were often viewed as celebrities. Gladiators were especially popular with women who admired their bravery and skill.

Even when not preparing for a contest, gladiators kept in shape by wrestling with the other gladiators at the training school.

We must stay in shape for the fight next week!

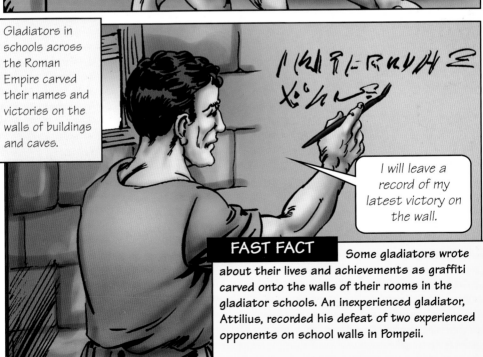

Gladiators in schools across the Roman Empire carved their names and victories on the walls of buildings and caves.

I will leave a record of my latest victory on the wall.

FAST FACT Some gladiators wrote about their lives and achievements as graffiti carved onto the walls of their rooms in the gladiator schools. An inexperienced gladiator, Attilius, recorded his defeat of two experienced opponents on school walls in Pompeii.

More victories brought a gladiator greater fame and larger fights. Famous fighters from Iberia (Spain) and Gaul (modern France, Belgium, and parts of Switzerland, the Netherlands and Germany) would be brought to Rome to fight against local champions.

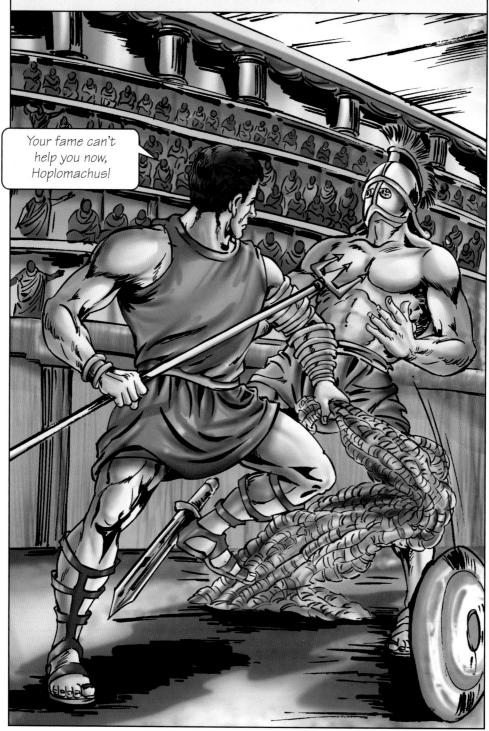

The fame and popularity of a particular gladiator could reach new heights if he were to fight successfully in front of the emperor and his family.

Roman Emperor Commodus was amazed by the skills of great gladiators. He would throw a laurel wreath crown to victorious gladiators as a sign of his pleasure.

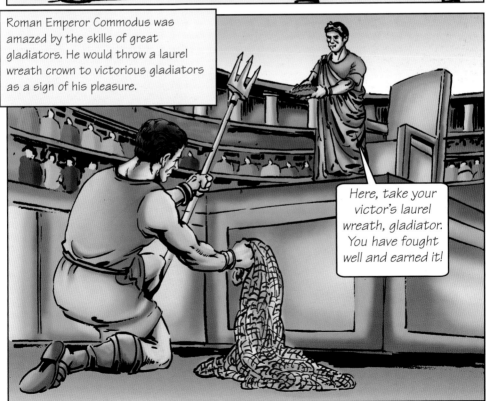

Emperor Commodus picked his favorite gladiators to appear in Rome's most extravagant shows, such as the reenactments of famous Roman navy sea battles.

Commodus would arrange for the Colosseum to be flooded. Then, great warships packed with soldiers would float into the arena to battle each other.

FAST FACT Historians disagree whether or not naumachia (mock sea battles) took place in the Colosseum. It was built on the marshy area of Emperor Nero's drained lake, so some historians believe the Colosseum could easily have been flooded and then emptied. Other historians believe there is no convincing evidence for this.

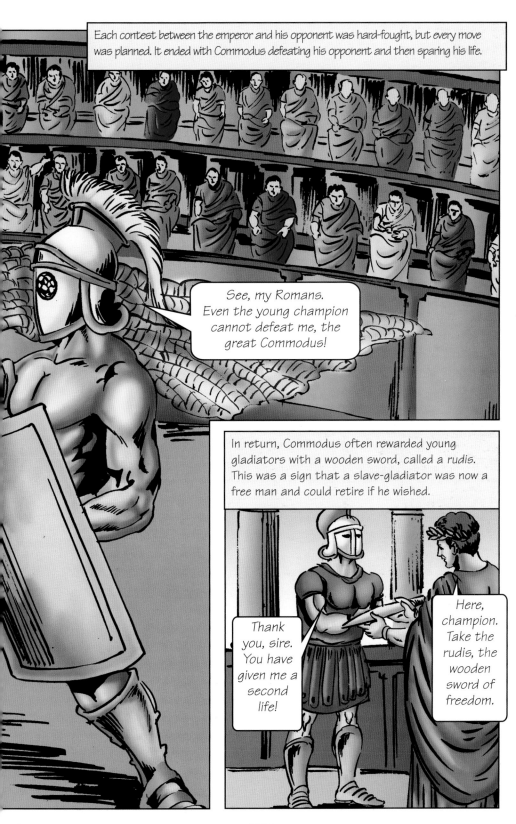

Each contest between the emperor and his opponent was hard-fought, but every move was planned. It ended with Commodus defeating his opponent and then sparing his life.

See, my Romans. Even the young champion cannot defeat me, the great Commodus!

In return, Commodus often rewarded young gladiators with a wooden sword, called a rudis. This was a sign that a slave-gladiator was now a free man and could retire if he wished.

Thank you, sire. You have given me a second life!

Here, champion. Take the rudis, the wooden sword of freedom.

CHRISTIANS IN THE ARENA

Famous gladiators sometimes survived the arena and retired to a new life as free men. Some were tempted back to fight, however, by a new cause—the persecution of Christians. Killing Christians in the Colosseum was popular until Constantine, Rome's first Christian emperor, came to power in A.D. 307. He ended this practice.

After retirement, many gladiators were happy to leave the bloodlust of the Colosseum's arena behind them.

Many returned to the Colosseum, however, to take part in the Roman persecution of Christians.

Wild beasts were brought from across the empire to attack and devour unarmed Christians. Spectators would roar their approval at the gruesome spectacle.

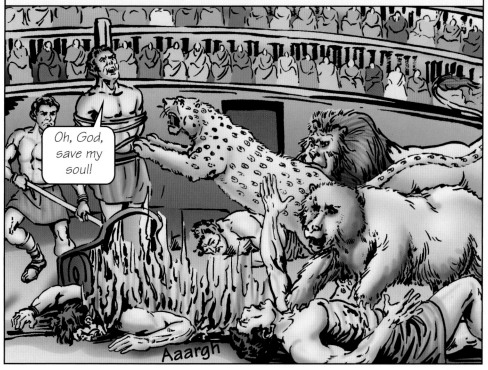

The main attraction of these shows was a fight between a gladiator and a Christian. The gladiator wore no armor, but used his skills, weapon, and net to fight against a Christian slave armed only with a useless dummy sword.

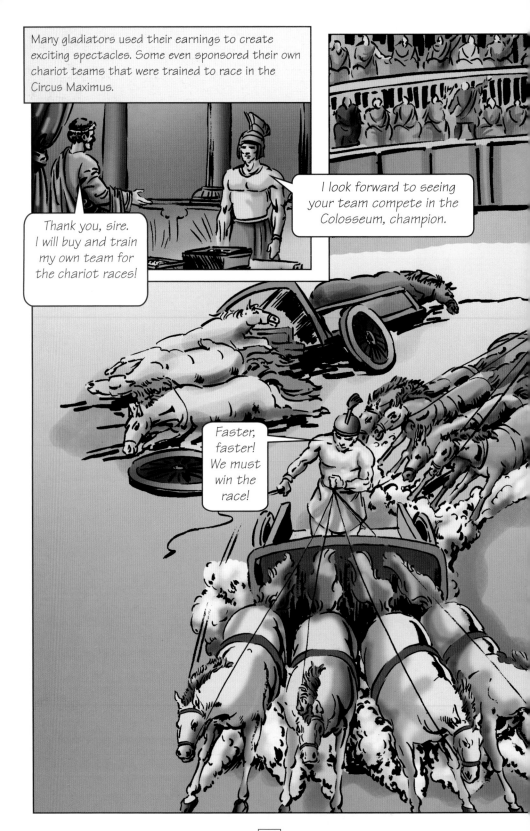

Many gladiators used their earnings to create exciting spectacles. Some even sponsored their own chariot teams that were trained to race in the Circus Maximus.

I look forward to seeing your team compete in the Colosseum, champion.

Thank you, sire. I will buy and train my own team for the chariot races!

Faster, faster! We must win the race!

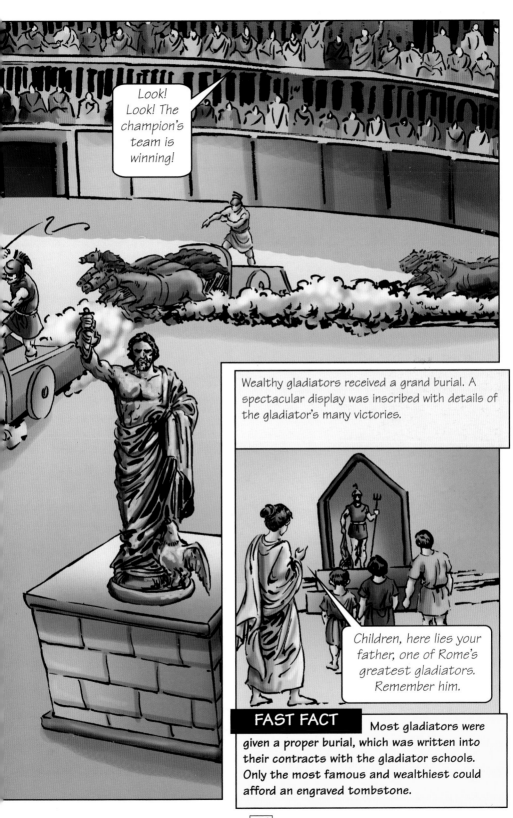

Look! Look! The champion's team is winning!

Wealthy gladiators received a grand burial. A spectacular display was inscribed with details of the gladiator's many victories.

Children, here lies your father, one of Rome's greatest gladiators. Remember him.

FAST FACT Most gladiators were given a proper burial, which was written into their contracts with the gladiator schools. Only the most famous and wealthiest could afford an engraved tombstone.

On August 23, A.D. 217, the Colosseum was struck by lightning and went up in flames. Large parts of the amphitheater had to be rebuilt over the next twenty years.

In A.D. 262, the Colosseum was seriously damaged again, this time by a great earthquake that struck Rome.

Once again, the Colosseum was repaired and rebuilt. It was ready for use by Emperor Aurelian, who held competitions and games in the arena in A.D. 274.

In A.D. 307, Constantine the Great became Rome's first Christian emperor. He banned the practice of allowing criminals and Christians to become gladiators, but he did not ban the gladiatorial contests.

Christianity is our new religion. All persecution of Christians must stop.

In A.D. 330, Constantine left Rome and established his new capital of Constantinople on the site of the old Greek city of Byzantium in Asia Minor (modern Turkey). His departure marked the beginning of the end of the Colosseum's gladiatorial games.

Keep Rome safe. I must sail to Constantinople, my new capital in the east.

SACKED AND ABANDONED

Rome suffered many disasters between the 5th and 8th centuries A.D. Earthquakes, fires, invasions, and mass emigrations of Romans to safer areas within the empire led to the city's decline. No longer in use, the Colosseum fell into disuse and was pillaged for its valuable building materials.

In A.D. 410, Rome was attacked by the invading Goths. They looted the Colosseum and left it abandoned for several years. It was not fully restored until A.D. 423.

Earthquakes and fires seriously damaged the Colosseum again between A.D. 429 and the end of the 5th century. By A.D. 545, only 500 civilians lived in Rome. The great Colosseum was again abandoned.

During the 6th and 7th centuries A.D., the Colosseum and other major Roman buildings were stripped of their marble, travertine, lead pipes, and iron clamps by the Roman people.

Here, take these iron clamps. We can sell them in the market.

They sold these items for money and food. During this time, many poor and homeless Romans lived beneath the arches of the Colosseum.

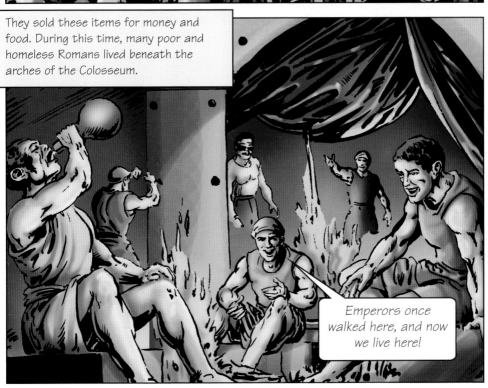

Emperors once walked here, and now we live here!

During early Medieval times, Rome was further damaged by earthquakes. After years of neglect, fires, and earthquakes, the Colosseum was in ruins.

What a fine home this will make for the mighty Frangipane family!

In A.D. 1084, Rome was conquered by the Normans. Eventually the Colosseum, along with many other great Roman buildings, was turned into a fortified house for one of Rome's noble families, the Frangipane family.

In later Medieval times, the Colosseum was pillaged again for building materials. During the 15th century, Pope Nicholas V took huge amounts of stone from the Colosseum to rebuild parts of the Vatican.

The stone in this building belongs to the Vatican now!

TOUR THE COLOSSEUM

The Colosseum was designed to hold up to 50,000 spectators. It had about 80 entrances, which enabled crowds to arrive and leave easily and quickly. Very little of the original building survives today. Archeologists believe that when it was first built, it would have looked like the illustration below.

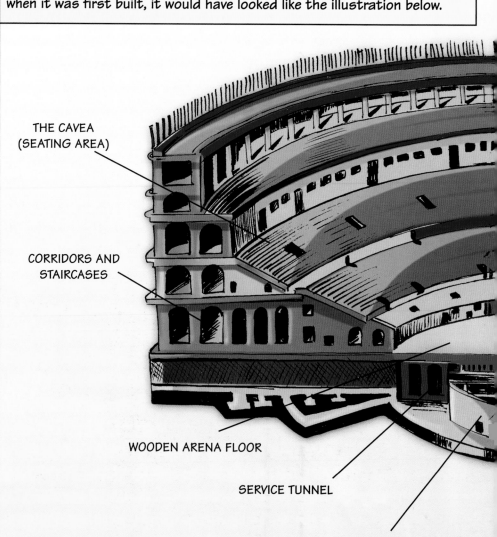

THE CAVEA
(SEATING AREA)

CORRIDORS AND
STAIRCASES

WOODEN ARENA FLOOR

SERVICE TUNNEL

UNDERGROUND ROOMS FOR
ANIMAL CAGES, PRISON CELLS,
AND STOREROOMS

FAST FACT Recent investigations have shown that the Colosseum and other amphitheaters had dozens of trap doors and lifts for moving animals, gladiators, and scenery into and out of the arena.

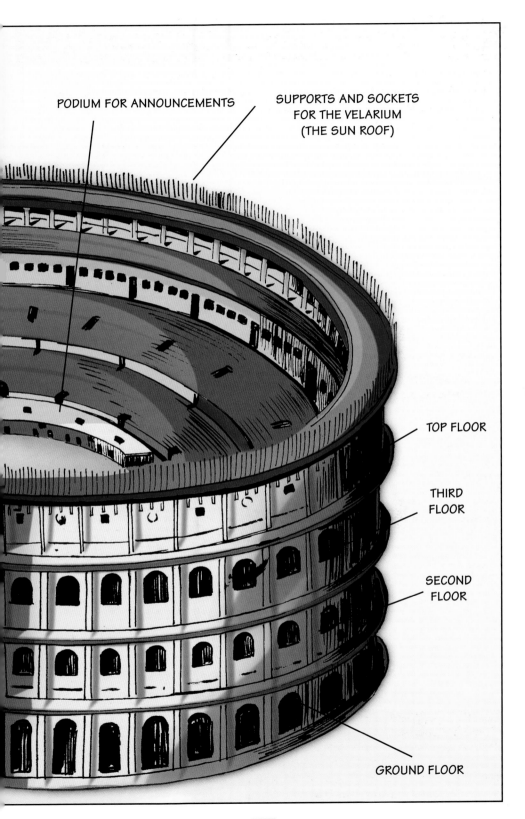

PODIUM FOR ANNOUNCEMENTS

SUPPORTS AND SOCKETS
FOR THE VELARIUM
(THE SUN ROOF)

TOP FLOOR

THIRD
FLOOR

SECOND
FLOOR

GROUND FLOOR

The Colosseum began as Emperor Vespasian's grand idea. Building on ancient Roman practices of staging fighting contests at funerals, gladiatorial contests in amphitheaters were established in Rome by the 3rd century B.C. However, the Colosseum's fortunes declined as Rome lost power.

753 B.C.: *The founding of Rome.*

264 B.C.: *The first gladiatorial battle is staged in Rome.*

200 B.C.: *The term* gladiator *first appears in the writings of the Roman author Cato.*

73–71 B.C.: *Spartacus, a slave-gladiator, rebels against Rome.*

70 B.C.: *The amphitheater at Pompeii is built.*

45 B.C.: *Julius Caesar becomes dictator of Rome.*

27 B.C.: *Octavian becomes Augustus, the first Roman emperor.*

A.D. 69: *Emperor Vespasian commissions the building of the Colosseum.*

A.D. 80: *Emperor Titus opens the Colosseum.*

A.D. 98–117: *During the reign of Emperor Trajan, the first Christian martyrs are killed by animals in the Colosseum.*

A.D. 192: *Emperor Commodus famously kills hundreds of wild beasts in the Colosseum.*

A.D. 217: *A lightning strike causes a disastrous fire at the Colosseum. It takes 20 years to repair the damage. During this time, the games take place in the Circus Maximus.*

A.D. 326: *Christian Emperor Constantine makes recruiting gladiators more difficult, but he does not abolish gladiatorial shows.*

A.D. 365: *Emperor Valentinian I prohibits sentencing Christians to die in the Colosseum and other arenas, but he allows gladiatorial contests to continue until the end of the 4th century.*

A.D. 400: *The last known gladiator fights occur in the Colosseum.*

A.D. 410: *Rome is sacked by the Goths.*

A.D. 417–423: *The Colosseum is restored after the Goths' retreat.*

A.D. 438: *All gladiatorial contests are banned by Emperor Valentinian III, but animal shows and public executions in the Colosseum continue.*

A.D. 500–700: *The Colosseum is stripped of its marble, lead pipes, and iron clamps by poor Romans, many of whom live in its remains.*

A.D. 1349: *An earthquake seriously damages the south and west sides of the Colosseum.*

A.D. 1440s: *Pope Nicholas V takes much of the stone from the Colosseum to rebuild the Basilica of St. Peter in the Vatican.*

A.D. 1749: *Pope Benedict XIV declares the Colosseum sanctified by the blood of the Christian martyrs, saving it from further pillaging.*

A.D. 1937: *The Ludus Magnus, Rome's main gladiator school, is discovered next to the Colosseum.*

DID YOU KNOW?

1. The earliest Roman amphitheaters date to the late 2nd century B.C. and are located at Capua, Cumae, and Liternum in southwest Italy.

2. The best-preserved early Roman amphitheater is in Pompeii. It was built around 70 B.C. and has remained intact because it was buried under volcanic ash when Mount Vesuvius erupted in A.D. 79.

3. The word amphitheater was first used in the 2nd century B.C. Before that, Romans used the term spectacula to describe the building and the contests that took place there.

4. Building the Colosseum according to Vespasian's design took 3.5 million cubic feet of travertine, 9 million cubic feet of mortar and aggregate to make the concrete, 330 tons of iron clamps, and 1 million bricks.

5. The Colosseum had 80 entrances, 76 of which were numbered (some are still visible today). The emperor's entrance on the south side was destroyed in the Middle Ages.

6. Gladiators entered through the western entrance, known as the Porta Triumphalis, and exited (alive or dead) through the eastern entrance, called the Porta Libitinensis (Gate of Death).

7. The awning, which protected the spectators from the sun, was supported by 240 poles. One thousand sailors from the Roman fleets operated the rigging system.

8. On the evening before a contest, gladiators would be put on display so that the public could examine them and decide whom to bet on the following day.

9. The paegniarii (comic gladiators) warmed up the audience before the real contests and during breaks between fights. They were actors disguised as gladiators and sometimes wore strange masks.

10. Galen, a founding father of modern medicine, began his career as a doctor in a gladiator school in A.D. 157. He later became the physician to several Roman emperors.

11. Roman women adored the gladiators, who were like celebrity superstars of the day. Rich senators' wives even sometimes ran off with their favorite gladiators.

12. The most famous gladiator was Spartacus, a Thracian, who led a gladiators' rebellion in 73–71 B.C. Spartacus' army of up to 100,000 disillusioned gladiators and slaves defeated many Roman armies until he was finally killed. His body was never found, and 6,000 of his rebels were crucified.

13. In wild beast shows, animals sometimes refused to fight or kill. Animal handlers provoked them, prodding them with spears or starving them, in order to make them perform for the crowds.

GLOSSARY

Amphitheater: *This word in Latin literally means a* double theatre, *where the seating surrounds the entire central arena, not just on one side.*

Arena: *This word means* sand *in Latin. Sand was spread onto the floor of amphitheaters to help absorb blood spilled from fighting.*

Bestiarii: *Gladiators who fought wild animals.*

Cavea: *The wooden or carved-stone seating area of an amphitheater.*

Christian: *Someone who believes in Jesus as Christ and follows the religion of Christianity based on the life and teachings of Jesus.*

Circus: *A long, oval stadium built especially for chariot racing. Rome's most famous example was the Circus Maximus.*

Consuls: *Rome's two consuls were the city's chief magistrates. They were elected each year.*

Crupellarius: *A heavily armed gladiator who was usually from Gaul (France).*

Equite*: A gladiator who fought on horseback.*

Essedarius*: A gladiator who fought in a chariot.*

Forum: *The political, legal, and commercial center of Rome, where* politicians addressed the people and business was conducted.

Gaul: *An ancient region of western Europe, south and west of the Rhine River, west of the Alps, and north of the Pyrenees. It corresponds roughly to modern-day France and Belgium. The Romans extended the area of Gaul to include northern Italy, particularly after Julius Caesar's conquest of the area in the Gallic Wars (58–51 B.C.).*

Gladius: *A short sword used by Roman soldiers and gladiators.*

Golden House*: The* Domus Aurea *was built by Emperor Nero in A.D. 64. Large sections were dismantled by Emperor Vespasian to build the Colosseum.*

Goth: *A member of the Germanic people who invaded the Roman Empire in the 3rd to 5th centuries A.D.*

Graffiti: *Words, and sometimes images, scratched or painted onto a wall.*

Greave: *A metal leg guard used by Roman soldiers and some gladiators.*

Hoplomachus: *A heavily-armored gladiator, possibly of Greek origin, who wore a helmet and was armed with an arm guard, greaves, a small circular shield, and a sword.*

Iberia: *A peninsula of southwest Europe that is now modern-day Spain and Portugal.*

GLOSSARY

Imperial: *Relating to an empire or an emperor or empress.*

Lanista: *A man who trained gladiators.*

Laurel wreath: *A crown made out of laurel leaves that is given as a prize to mark a victory.*

Ludus: *A school where gladiators trained. The Ludus Magnus was next to the Colosseum.*

Munus: *The easliest version of a gladiatorial contest as part of a funeral ritual to honor the memory of an important person.*

Murmillos: *Gladiators who wore large visored helmets and fought with a large, oblong shield and sword.*

Naumachia: *A mock naval battle which sometimes took place in an arena that had been specially flooded.*

Paegniarii: *Men with sticks who fought fake, and sometimes humorous, battles to entertain the crowd before the real fights began.*

Pilum: *A javelin used by Roman soldiers and gladiators.*

Plebian: *A members of the common, lower classes of Rome.*

Procurator: *The chief of a gladiator school. He was appointed by the emperor.*

Retiarius: *The lowest-ranking gladiator, who was lightly armed with a trident and a net.*

Rudis: *A wooden sword given to a gladiator on his retirement or as a symbol of his freedom.*

Samnite: *A gladiator who wore a visored helmet with a plume and was armed with a large shield and sword.*

Secutor: *A gladiator who was specially trained to fight a retiarius. Secutors wore a heavy helmet with only two small eye-holes designed to prevent injury from the retiarius' trident.*

Slave: *A man or woman who is owned by another person and does not have the rights of freedom.*

Thracian: *An especially popular kind of gladiator. Thracians were armed with a curved dagger and a small shield.*

Travertine: *White limestone widely used in Roman buildings, especially in the construction of the Colosseum.*

Trident: *A long, three-pronged fork used by retiarius gladiators*

Velarium: *The awning (removable roof covering) used to protect amphitheater spectators from the hot sun.*

Velites: *Roman soldiers and gladiators who were armed with javelins.*

INDEX